This Book Donated to
the Children of Placerville by
Mr. Gordon Purdy
Who Loved Children and
Books in That Order -
Usually.

ELLEN DeGENERES

GROUNDBREAKING ENTERTAINER

BY JILL C. WHEELER

CONTENT CONSULTANT

abdopublishing.com

Published by Abdo Publishing, a division of ABDO, PO Box 398166,
Minneapolis, Minnesota 55439. Copyright © 2018 by Abdo Consulting
Group, Inc. International copyrights reserved in all countries. No part of this
book may be reproduced in any form without written permission from the
publisher. Core Library™ is a trademark and logo of Abdo Publishing.

Printed in the United States of America, North Mankato, Minnesota
042017
092017

Cover Photo: Pablo Martinez Monsivais/AP Images
Interior Photos: Pablo Martinez Monsivais/AP Images, 1; Olivier Douliery/ABACA/Sipa/
AP Images, 4–5, 45; Walt Disney Studios Motion Pictures/Everett Collection, 7; Rex Features/
AP Images, 9; Jeff Bottari/Human Rights Campaign/AP Images, 12–13; Ron Galella/Wirelmage/
Getty Images, 15, 18–19; Shea Walsh/Axe/AP Images, 20–21; Shutterstock Images, 22; Kevin
Winter/Getty Images Entertainment/Getty Images, 26; Touchstone Television/Everett Collection,
28–29, 31; Kevork Djansezian/AP Images, 34–35; Can Nguyen/REX/AP Images, 37; Andrew Harnik/
AP Images, 39; Red Line Editorial, 40

Editor: Heidi Schoof
Imprint Designer: Maggie Villaume
Series Design Direction: Maggie Villaume

Publisher's Cataloging-in-Publication Data

Names: Wheeler, Jill C., author.
Title: Ellen DeGeneres : groundbreaking entertainer / by Jill C. Wheeler.
Other titles: Groundbreaking entertainer
Description: Minneapolis, MN : Abdo Publishing, 2018. | Series: Newsmakers |
    Includes bibliographical references and index.
Identifiers: LCCN 2017930422 | ISBN 9781532111822 (lib. bdg.) |
    ISBN 9781680789676 (ebook)
Subjects: LCSH: DeGeneres, Ellen--Juvenile literature. | Comedians--United
    States--Biography--Juvenile literature. | Television personalities--United
    States--Biography--Juvenile literature.
Classification: DDC 792.702 [B]--dc23
LC record available at http://lccn.loc.gov/2017930422

CONTENTS

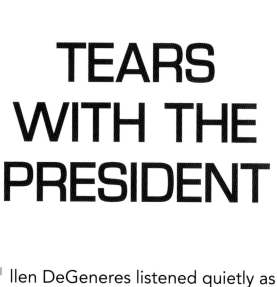

TEARS WITH THE PRESIDENT

Ellen DeGeneres listened quietly as President Barack Obama spoke of her courage. She listened as Obama praised her ability to make people laugh about something rather than laughing at someone. She listened as he told the White House audience how DeGeneres always reminded people to be nice to one another. Then, when Obama placed the Presidential Medal of Freedom around her neck, she cried.

Ellen DeGeneres received the Medal of Freedom from President Barack Obama in a special ceremony in the East Room of the White House.

THE PRESIDENTIAL MEDAL OF FREEDOM

The Presidential Medal of Freedom is the highest non-military honor in the United States. The award recognizes people for their contributions to culture, the nation, and the world. DeGeneres shared the 2016 stage with several notable Medal of Freedom recipients. They included actors Tom Hanks and Robert DeNiro, musician Bruce Springsteen, athletes Kareem Abdul-Jabbar and Michael Jordan, and philanthropists Bill and Melinda Gates.

DeGeneres was one of 21 Americans honored with the Medal of Freedom in November 2016. The comedian has spent a lifetime making people laugh. She has worked to create an equal and more loving world for humans and animals. She has received many honors and awards for her work in television, movies, and stand-up comedy. DeGeneres was introduced to young audiences as the voice of Dory in the animated movies *Finding Nemo* and *Finding Dory*. Dory, a fish, reminded audiences of the power of kindness and of never giving up.

The role of Dory, a forgetful but lovable fish, was written with DeGeneres in mind.

DeGeneres earned the Medal of Freedom for her influence on society. The host of the awards ceremony summed it up well. He said DeGeneres taught us that each of us can make the world a more fun, open, and loving place. All we have to do is "just keep swimming."

WORKING FOR MARRIAGE EQUALITY

The Medal of Freedom ceremony was not the first time President Obama thanked DeGeneres. The president appeared on *The Ellen DeGeneres Show* in February 2016. He complimented DeGeneres for speaking out on the issue of same-sex marriage.

Obama spoke about DeGeneres's decision to talk openly about being a lesbian. He noted how that decision had helped pave the way for same-sex marriage rights. He said that her being willing to be herself gave others power.

A FOCUS ON THE POSITIVE

DeGeneres has had a successful and groundbreaking career. She was among the first celebrities to publicly acknowledge that she is a lesbian. This was before being gay became more widely accepted. Her relationships with women captured tabloid headlines just as her acting, comedy, and writing captured laughs.

DeGeneres uses her dancing to make people smile. Many visitors to *The Ellen DeGeneres Show* share a dance with Ellen—including First Lady Michelle Obama.

She has remained above it all by focusing on the positive. She emphasizes the power of laughter and kindness to change hearts and minds.

Of course, no event would be complete without at least some humor from the comedy star. There was a mix-up with DeGeneres's photo identification on the day of the awards. No one is allowed inside the White House without a photo ID. That meant DeGeneres had to wait outside until the issue was resolved. She made light of the situation as she often does: "They haven't let me in to the White House yet because I forgot my ID," she tweeted. "Not joking."

After the ceremony, she posed for photos with her spouse of eight years, actress Portia de Rossi. Once again, DeGeneres tweeted: "Barack Obama just awarded me the Medal of Freedom. I hope it serves as an ID. I have no idea how I'm getting home."

STRAIGHT TO THE
SOURCE

DeGeneres has been honored for her work promoting equal rights. She was recognized for this work at the 2015 Teen Choice Awards. She gave the following remarks when she accepted her Choice Comedian award:

> I want to say also it feels good to be chosen, but there was a time in my life that I was not chosen. I was the opposite of chosen because I was different, and I think I want to make sure that everyone knows that what makes you different right now, makes you stand out later in life. So you should be proud of being different, proud of who you are. . . . The most important thing I want to say is just really embrace who you are because being unique is very, very important and fitting in is not all that matters. It's being unique and being who you are.

> Source: Hayley Miller. "Ellen DeGeneres Gives Inspiring Speech to LGBTQ Youth." *Human Rights Campaign*. HRC, August 18, 2015. Web. Accessed January 13, 2017.

What's the Big Idea?

Take a close look at this passage. What does DeGeneres say about accepting yourself for who you are? Pick out two details she uses to make her point. What do you notice about the way she uses the word *chosen*?

FINDING A VOICE

Ellen Lee DeGeneres was born on January 26, 1958, in Metairie, Louisiana. Metairie is located near New Orleans. Her mother, Betty, was an administrative assistant. Her father, Elliott, was an insurance agent. Ellen grew up with one older brother, Vance. Vance DeGeneres is also a comedian and actor. The family raised Ellen and her brother in the Christian Science religion until Ellen was 13 years old.

Growing up, no one would have guessed that Ellen would be a comedian. She was a quiet, reserved child. Her brother was considered the funny one in the family.

Betty DeGeneres, mother of Ellen DeGeneres, speaks at an event in support of LGBTQ youth.

WHAT IS CHRISTIAN SCIENCE?

Christian Science is a religion that teaches that all sickness and injury can be healed through prayer. Growing up, Ellen and her brother did not even use aspirin or other painkillers.

Ellen later said she sometimes felt like an outsider because of the religion. When all the other kids lined up for vaccinations, she didn't have to. That was because she was a Christian Scientist. Ellen stopped participating in the religion after her parents' divorce.

The DeGeneres family moved around a lot because of Elliott's job. Ellen remembers how it felt to always be new. She says she just wanted to feel like she belonged. Later she used those feelings to make up jokes for her comedy routine. She knew other people could relate to them, too.

Ellen's comedic abilities began to surface in her teen years. Her parents separated in 1972 and divorced in 1974. Ellen recalls seeing her mother upset after the divorce. She would make fun of Betty's dancing to cheer her up. Once Betty was laughing, Ellen

Vance DeGeneres accompanies his sister to the 1995 Golden Globe Awards. Vance is an actor, comedian, musician, screenwriter, and producer.

would imitate her laughing. Betty would start to cry from laughing so hard.

UNWANTED MOVE

Betty DeGeneres made a sudden decision when her daughter was a junior in high school. By then, Betty had married a man named Roy Gruessendorf. Vance was already on his own. Betty decided to move herself, Roy, and Ellen to Atlanta, Texas. This news hit Ellen hard.

She did not want to leave her friends. Nor did she want to leave the city and move to a rural area. Ellen threatened to move in with her grandmother who lived in New Orleans. Betty took her on a visit to Atlanta to try to change her mind. Once there, she pointed out the positive things in the small city. Betty's plan worked, and the family moved to Texas.

Ellen graduated from Atlanta High School in 1976. She packed her car and left for Louisiana the day after her graduation.

TRAGEDY TO COMEDY

While Ellen was living in New Orleans, she was in a relationship. Ellen was 19 when her girlfriend was killed in a car accident. She recalls driving by the accident scene. Later she learned the victim's identity.

Ellen was living in a flea-infested basement apartment with no heat, no air conditioning, and a mattress on the floor. She began to wonder why bad things happen to people. She thought it would be nice if she could telephone God to get answers. The comedy bit she wrote about such a phone call would help her make history as a comedian.

She was going to stay with her grandmother and study at the University of New Orleans. She began taking classes in communications studies but soon dropped out. She stayed in New Orleans and supported herself with a variety of odd jobs. These included working as a restaurant hostess, a house painter, and a bartender. Yet none of them really fit her personality. Ellen realized she wanted a job where she didn't have to follow someone else's rules. As it turned out, comedy was perfect for that.

FURTHER EVIDENCE

Chapter Two includes information about DeGeneres's personality. What was one of the chapter's main points? What evidence was given to support that point? Go to the article about DeGeneres at the website below. Does the information in this article support an existing piece of evidence in the chapter? Does it add new evidence?

ELLEN DEGENERES: EQUAL PARTS COMEDIAN AND HUMANITARIAN

abdocorelibrary.com/ellen-degeneres

CHAPTER
THREE

STAND-UP SUCCESS

DeGeneres began creating her own stand-up routine in her early twenties. She started small. She would come home from one of her many jobs and write short, funny bits. She didn't know whether she would ever perform them. When she did begin performing, it was for her friends. She performed at coffee shops or small comedy clubs. She would do comedy at night and work during the day. Because she was funny, her name soon got around.

The owner of an up-and-coming comedy club in New Orleans heard about DeGeneres's act. The club, Clyde's Comedy Club, hired her

DeGeneres built a successful stand-up comedy career in the 1980s.

DeGeneres performed her act at comedy clubs, like the Laugh Factory in Hollywood, California.

as the opener. Soon, she was making enough money doing comedy that she did not have to work a day job.

It was DeGeneres's responsibility as the opener to put the audience in a good mood. She was given

less than ten minutes onstage to do that. DeGeneres
worked her way up from opening. Eventually she had a
full hour onstage. She also began to work as an emcee,
or master of ceremonies, introducing other acts.

KEY PLACES IN DeGENERES'S EARLY LIFE

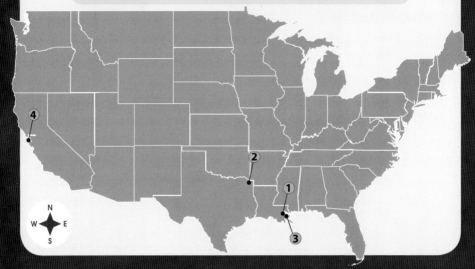

1. Born in Metairie, Louisiana
2. Moved to Atlanta, Texas, while in high school
3. Moved to New Orleans, Louisiana, after graduation
4. Moved to San Francisco, California, to pursue comedy career

Ellen DeGeneres lived and worked in several cities before she became a famous comedian. How does the information presented compare with what you have learned from the text about her early life? How do you think her life and surroundings might have differed for DeGeneres in each of these places?

CALIFORNIA DREAMING

DeGeneres did well at Clyde's. Yet the club was one of only a few comedy venues in New Orleans. DeGeneres knew she would need to move if she wanted to make it big. She took a friend's advice and moved to San

Francisco, California. The city was full of comedy clubs. That made it even more challenging for DeGeneres. She struggled to stand out from the many funny people working in the city. After a few months, she returned to New Orleans. She was broke and homesick. She also discovered that Clyde's had closed while she was gone. She found herself once again working odd jobs and scraping by in a flea-infested apartment.

Then her life changed. In 1982, DeGeneres sent an audition tape to the Showtime TV network's Funniest Person in America competition. Later that same year, DeGeneres got a call telling her she had been named Showtime's Funniest Person in Louisiana. Not long after, she competed for the national title and won. DeGeneres was named the Funniest Person in America.

She then moved back to San Francisco. Moving there the second time was much easier. DeGeneres's national recognition landed her a gig at the elite Improv Club. The Improv Club attracted many talent scouts, producers, and directors. There DeGeneres met the man who would become one of her biggest supporters. He was superstar comedian Jay Leno. DeGeneres opened for Leno at the Improv Club. Leno loved her comedic style. A few years later he would help DeGeneres fulfill one of her biggest dreams. He helped her get the chance to perform for Johnny Carson on *The Tonight Show* in 1986.

MAKING HISTORY ON *THE TONIGHT SHOW*

Comedians dreamed of performing on *The Tonight Show,* hosted by Johnny Carson from 1962 to 1992. They also dreamed of being invited to sit and talk with Carson on the show afterward. No one knew in advance who would be invited to sit with him. Carson had never invited a female comedian to do so.

THE TONIGHT SHOW

The Tonight Show is a long-running late-night talk show that began in New York City in 1954. The show features monologues, musical acts, celebrity interviews, and comedy skits.

Steve Allen hosted the show for the first three years. Jack Parr followed as host for the next five years. Johnny Carson took over the job on October 1, 1962. Carson's likable personality quickly earned him the title "the king of late night." He hosted *The Tonight Show Starring Johnny Carson* for 30 years. Carson retired in May 1992. Comedian Jay Leno was chosen to take his place. Jimmy Fallon became the host when Leno retired in 2014.

After her routine, DeGeneres waited a moment to look over at Carson. She saw him laughing and motioning for her to come join him. She had made history. DeGeneres was the first and only woman to be invited to chat with Carson after her first appearance on the show.

STRAIGHT TO THE
SOURCE

DeGeneres made history when she impressed Johnny Carson with a stand-up performance on his show. She described the inspiration for her "Phone Call to God" routine during an interview for the *New York Times*:

> *I'm laying on the floor, wide awake, thinking, "Here's this beautiful girl, 23 years old, who's just gone" . . . So I started writing what it would be like to call God and ask why fleas are here and this person is not.*

> *But my mind just kicked into what . . . would happen if you actually picked up the phone and called God. How it would take forever, how it would ring for a long time because . . . it's a big place.*

> Source: Bill Carter. "At Lunch With: Ellen DeGeneres; Dialed God (Pause). He Laughed." *New York Times*. New York Times, April 13, 1994. Web. Accessed March 15, 2017.

Point of View
Comedians often take a specific point of view in their stand-up routines. What point of view does DeGeneres take when she is thinking about this routine? How do you think she hopes to relate to her audiences?

ELLEN

By 1988, DeGeneres had established herself in the world of stand-up comedy. Now she was ready for a change of pace. A stand-up career meant spending 300 or more days of the year on the road. It meant performing in many different cities. Sometimes when opening a show, she would forget the name of the town she was in. DeGeneres turned even that into a joke. When introducing a show, instead of saying "How are you doing, South Bend?" she might open with "Hey there, East Berlin!"

DeGeneres wanted to do something that would let her stay in one place for longer periods of time. She started exploring her

In the 1990s, Ellen DeGeneres turned her attention to acting.

29

DeGENERES THE AUTHOR

Throughout her career, DeGeneres has taken the time to share her wit and wisdom in books as well as on stage and screen. Her first book was *My Point . . . And I Do Have One*. It is a collection of comic essays and was published in 1995.

In 2003, DeGeneres published a second book. *The Funny Thing Is . . .* features DeGeneres's funny comments on everything from fashion trends to how to handle seating arrangements at a celebrity brunch. Her 2011 book *Seriously . . . I'm Kidding* includes more comic observations. DeGeneres wrote another book in 2015, titled *Home*. It focuses on her experiences in buying and renovating homes.

options for acting on television. She briefly appeared on two sitcoms, *Open House* and *Laurie Hill*. Then, in 1994, DeGeneres got her own show. It was called *These Friends of Mine*. In its second season, *These Friends of Mine* really took off. At that time, the show was renamed *Ellen*. Audiences fell in love with DeGeneres's goofy sense of humor. She was nominated for four Emmy Awards for her role on the show.

In the two-part "Puppy Episode," Ellen's character realizes she is gay and eventually comes out to her friends.

By the fourth season of *Ellen*, DeGeneres wanted her character to do something important. It was something that she herself had done only to her mother and a few friends. That something was to come out as a lesbian. It would make her the first lead sitcom character in history to say that she was gay.

TAKING CHANCES

DeGeneres knew it was a risky move. She was scared about how her audience would react. She feared that her fans would no longer applaud or laugh. She worried they would no longer like her if they knew she was gay. As it turned out, more than 46 million people watched the show. DeGeneres won her first Emmy for writing the episode.

DeGeneres received many positive letters about her character's bravery. She received a lot of opposition, too. *Ellen* began to lose viewers. Many of those who

A DIFFICULT CHOICE

Not long before the coming-out episode of *Ellen*, DeGeneres came out on the cover of *Time* magazine in 1997. Before *Time*, DeGeneres had told only a few people that she was gay. She had told her mother when she was 19. She and Betty were walking on a beach when DeGeneres said she was in love. Her mother said that was great. Then DeGeneres told her who it was. Although she was surprised, Betty was extremely supportive.

left complained that the show focused too much on Ellen's character being gay. Some advertisers refused to have their commercials appear on the show. Executives with the show's network, ABC, were also nervous that they would offend some viewers. They began showing a warning message before every episode that showed DeGeneres dating another woman. The message warned parents that the show contained adult content. ABC cancelled the show in 1998.

EXPLORE ONLINE

Chapter Four focuses on DeGeneres coming out very publicly as gay. The website below has even more information about this event and its effect on her life and career. As you know, every source is different. What are the similarities between Chapter Four and the information you found on the website? Are there any differences? How do the two sources present information differently?

ELLEN DEGENERES: MY JOB'S TO MAKE YOU HAPPY
abdocorelibrary.com/ellen-degeneres

STARTING OVER

Suddenly, DeGeneres had nowhere to work. No one wanted to hire her as an actor. It would be three years before her phone rang for a part.

DeGeneres was upset. But there was also positive news. She was getting letters from kids around the country who were gay. The kids told her that seeing *Ellen* gave them new hope for the future.

Since she could not be on-screen, DeGeneres decided to go back to where it all began. She returned to the stage and to stand-up. Her jokes were still clean and smart.

Ellen DeGeneres returned to making people smile as host of the 2001 Emmy Awards.

HOSTING THE 2001 EMMY AWARDS

DeGeneres was given the honor of hosting the 2001 Emmy Awards. The show took place less than two months after the September 11, 2001, terrorist attacks on the World Trade Center and the Pentagon. DeGeneres would have to be funny. She would also have to be respectful of the recent tragedy and loss of life.

DeGeneres more than met the challenge. She received several standing ovations. That appearance also marked the beginning of her comedy comeback.

Audiences still loved her. In 2001, she returned to television briefly on a sitcom called *The Ellen Show.* It did not last long. Yet it became clear that DeGeneres was in the business to stay.

DeGeneres took on a 35-city stand-up tour in 2003. She also published her second book, *The Funny Thing Is . . . .* Then she lent her voice to the character of Dory in Pixar's hit movie *Finding Nemo.* Audiences fell in love with Dory, a blue tang fish who suffers from short-term memory loss. The role was written specifically for DeGeneres. *Finding Nemo*

DeGeneres posed for photos with her wife, Portia de Rossi, at the premiere of *Finding Dory*, the sequel to *Finding Nemo*, in 2016.

became one of the highest grossing animated movies of all time.

By the end of 2003, DeGeneres had landed yet another show named after her. This time though, things would be different. She would still be the star. But this show was not a sitcom. *The Ellen DeGeneres Show* was a talk show.

HUMOROUS HOST

The Ellen DeGeneres Show went on to become one of history's most awarded daytime talk shows. It won the Daytime Emmy for Outstanding Talk Show the first year it was nominated. On the show, DeGeneres has hosted countless celebrities, including Michelle Obama, Taylor Swift, and Justin Bieber. The show is upbeat and goofy, just like DeGeneres. DeGeneres will often prank her guests and encourage audience members to participate. The show has been running since September 2003. By early 2017, it had won 35 Daytime Emmy Awards, and it showed no signs of stopping.

DeGeneres also uses her celebrity status to support causes that are important to her. One of those causes is animal rights. DeGeneres is a vegan. She has

DeGeneres laughs while hosting *The Ellen DeGeneres Show* in 2016.

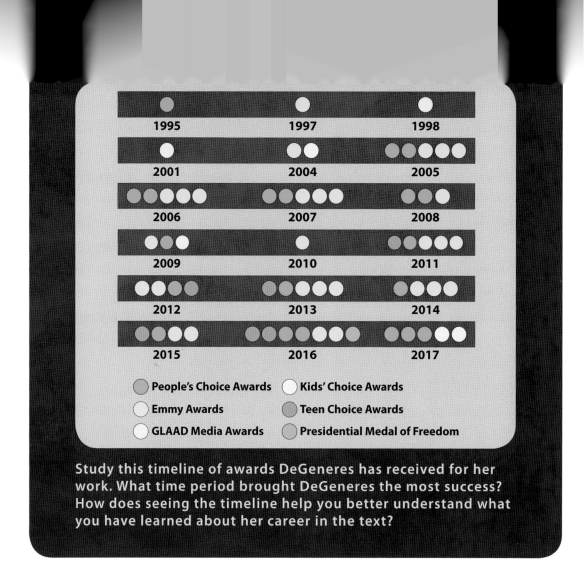

1995	1997	1998
2001	2004	2005
2006	2007	2008
2009	2010	2011
2012	2013	2014
2015	2016	2017

People's Choice Awards

Emmy Awards

GLAAD Media Awards

Kids' Choice Awards

Teen Choice Awards

Presidential Medal of Freedom

Study this timeline of awards DeGeneres has received for her work. What time period brought DeGeneres the most success? How does seeing the timeline help you better understand what you have learned about her career in the text?

a special page devoted to healthful recipes on her talk show website. Most of those recipes are vegan. The recipes encourage people to prepare meatless meals. In 2009, the activist group People for the Ethical Treatment of Animals (PETA) named DeGeneres their Woman of the Year. The honor recognized how

DeGeneres had used her popularity to talk about animal rights. She has also been recognized for her work against bullying.

In 2008, California legalized same-sex marriage. DeGeneres was able to marry her longtime girlfriend, actress Portia de Rossi. DeGeneres's courage in coming out as gay had helped change people's views. Because of that, she and many others could truly be themselves.

DeGENERES'S FASHION SENSE

DeGeneres has adopted a signature style. Her favorite outfit is a fashionable blazer, vest, pants, and tennis shoes. She says she dresses only to please herself.

She even has used her clothes to make people laugh. In 2006, she was giving a commencement address at Tulane University in New Orleans. She showed up in a bathrobe and slippers. The crowd was dressed in graduation caps and gowns. DeGeneres looked around and said, "They told me everyone would be wearing robes."

IMPORTANT
DATES

1958

DeGeneres is born in Metairie, Louisiana, to Elliott and Betty DeGeneres.

1972

Elliott and Betty DeGeneres separate and later divorce.

1976

DeGeneres graduates from high school in Atlanta, Texas.

1982

DeGeneres enters and wins a contest to be named the Funniest Person in America.

1986

After performing on *The Tonight Show with Johnny Carson*, DeGeneres becomes the first female comedian to be invited to sit and talk with Carson on the couch.

1994

DeGeneres gets her first successful television sitcom job on *These Friends of Mine*. The show is renamed *Ellen* in the second season.

1997
DeGeneres comes out as gay on the cover of
Time magazine.

2001
DeGeneres hosts the Emmy Awards just months after the
September 11th terrorist attacks.

2003
Audiences fall in love with DeGeneres as Dory in *Finding
Nemo*. DeGeneres gets her own daytime talk show titled
simply *The Ellen DeGeneres Show*.

2008
DeGeneres marries her longtime girlfriend Portia de Rossi.

2009
People for the Ethical Treatment of Animals (PETA) names
DeGeneres their Woman of the Year for using her celebrity
status to talk about animal rights issues.

2015
DeGeneres steps out of her typical comedy writing
to publish the book *Home*. The book is about her
experiences in buying and renovating homes.

STOP AND
THINK

Dig Deeper

After reading this book, what questions do you still have about Ellen DeGeneres? Do you want to learn more about stand-up comedy? Write down one or two questions that can guide you in doing research. With an adult's help, find a few reliable sources that can help answer your questions. Write a few sentences about how you did your research and what you learned from it.

Say What?

Comedians like DeGeneres have unique words to describe parts of their job. Find five words in this book that are new to you, or that have different meanings to people in the entertainment world than they do to most people. Use a dictionary to find out what they mean. Then write the meanings in your own words, and use each word in a new sentence.

Take a Stand

DeGeneres became a comedian in part because she wanted to be her own boss. What other careers let people be their own boss? Do you want to work for yourself someday? Or would you rather work for someone else? Which do you think is best, and why?

Tell the Tale

DeGeneres has made a career of being funny. What does it take to be funny? Write 200 words that tell a story from your life in such a way that it will make your friends laugh. Be sure to set the scene, develop a sequence of events, and offer a conclusion.

GLOSSARY

bit
a small part of a comedy routine or stage performance

elite
belonging to the most successful or powerful group

Emmy
a trophy awarded each year for excellence in American television

gay
a person who is attracted to people of the same sex

gig
a job for a musician or other entertainer

lesbian
a woman who is attracted to other women

opener
the first performance in a series of performances

philanthropist
a wealthy person who donates money and time

sitcom
a comedy show with a regular group of characters

stand-up
performing a comedy routine alone on a stage

vaccination
an injection that helps the body protect itself against a specific disease

vegan
a person who eats only food from plants and who often will avoid using animal products such as leather

LEARN
MORE

Books

Orr, Tamara. *Ellen DeGeneres.* Kennett Square, PA: Purple Toad Publishing, 2016.

Sharp, Katie John. *Ellen DeGeneres.* Detroit, MI: Lucent Books, 2010.

Simons, Rae. *Ellen DeGeneres.* New York: Village Earth Press, 2016.

Websites

To learn more about Newsmakers, visit **abdobooklinks.com**. These links are routinely monitored and updated to provide the most current information available.

Visit **abdocorelibrary.com** for free additional tools for teachers and students.

INDEX

About the Author

Jill C. Wheeler is the author of nearly 300 nonfiction books for young readers, covering everything from science and environmental topics to biographies of celebrities. Wheeler lives in Minneapolis, Minnesota, with her husband and whichever of their three adult daughters happens to be visiting at the time.